Beautiful Vintage Flowers
A Grayscale Coloring Book for Adults

Dar Payment

The Amazing Grayscale Coloring Company
Lake Elsinore, CA USA

Book design and cover art
By Dar Payment

Photographs sourced from Pixabay and PublicDomainPictures.net

Copyright © 2017 by Dar Payment

All rights reserved. No part of this book may be reproduced, stored in a retrieval system or transmitted, in any form or by any means, electronic, mechanical, photocopying, recording or otherwise, without the prior written consent from the author.

ISBN-13: 978-1974676873

Published by:

The Amazing Grayscale Coloring Company
A Division of DAP Publishing
Lake Elsinore, California USA

www.AmazingGrayscale.com

A Note from the Author

It was not my original intention to put together a coloring book. I am not a professional artist, but I love to color grayscale! And to be honest, the grayscale coloring selection I have shared with you in the following pages of this book are from one of my own private collections.

About a year ago I became totally fascinated with every aspect of coloring – especially with projects concerning grayscale. I was so excited that I began to host small coloring parties with my friends, offering many of the grayscale pages appearing in this book for our coloring inspirations.

My friends loved the coloring projects. Soon they were hooked and told me they wanted more similar grayscale pages to color!

These friends would often show their finished coloring projects with their friends, who wanted to color too . . . and well, the rest is joyful providence. The cumulation of the grayscale coloring book you are now holding in your hands.

Have fun bringing the images to life by filling them up with tons of beautiful color. And if you become obsessed with coloring like I did (and still am) and want to spread the love of coloring with your friends too, host your own coloring party using the pages of this book!

Blessings and Happy Coloring,

Dar Payment

"I prefer living in color." ~ David Hockney

How to Color Grayscale

Coloring grayscale is very easy, and there are a few schools of thought out there about how to color a grayscale image or photograph.

The number one thing about coloring grayscale is that the shading is already there for you which means no more trying to figure out where your light source or shadows need to be, etc..

The first grayscale coloring method is to use one color over each area first using very light pressure over the entire area you wish to color. Next, using the same color apply heavier pressure in the darker shaded areas.

Another method is to simply use your darkest colors to color over the areas with the heaviest gray shading. Then your lighter colors over the areas with the lightest gray shading, and finally using your medium colors to blend both the light and dark colors.

The point is that there is no wrong or right way to color grayscale. So have fun experimenting as you unleash your inner colorist, and enjoy watching as your photo or image comes to life before your eyes.

Need samples of coloring inspirations for the images in this book? Download a free full colored template containing all of the coloring inspirations depicted in this book at: https://www.amazinggrayscale.com/Free-Downloads.php

The Best Artist Mediums for This Book

The best artist mediums for this book are colored pencils. You can experiment with gel pens and markers if you'd like, but gel pens and markers will bleed through the page.

If you do choose to use gel pens or markers the best practice is to put a piece of paper underneath your coloring project in order to protect from bleed through onto the coloring page underneath it.

"Mere color, unspoiled by meaning, and unallied with definite form, can speak to the soul in a thousand different ways".

~ Oscar Wilde

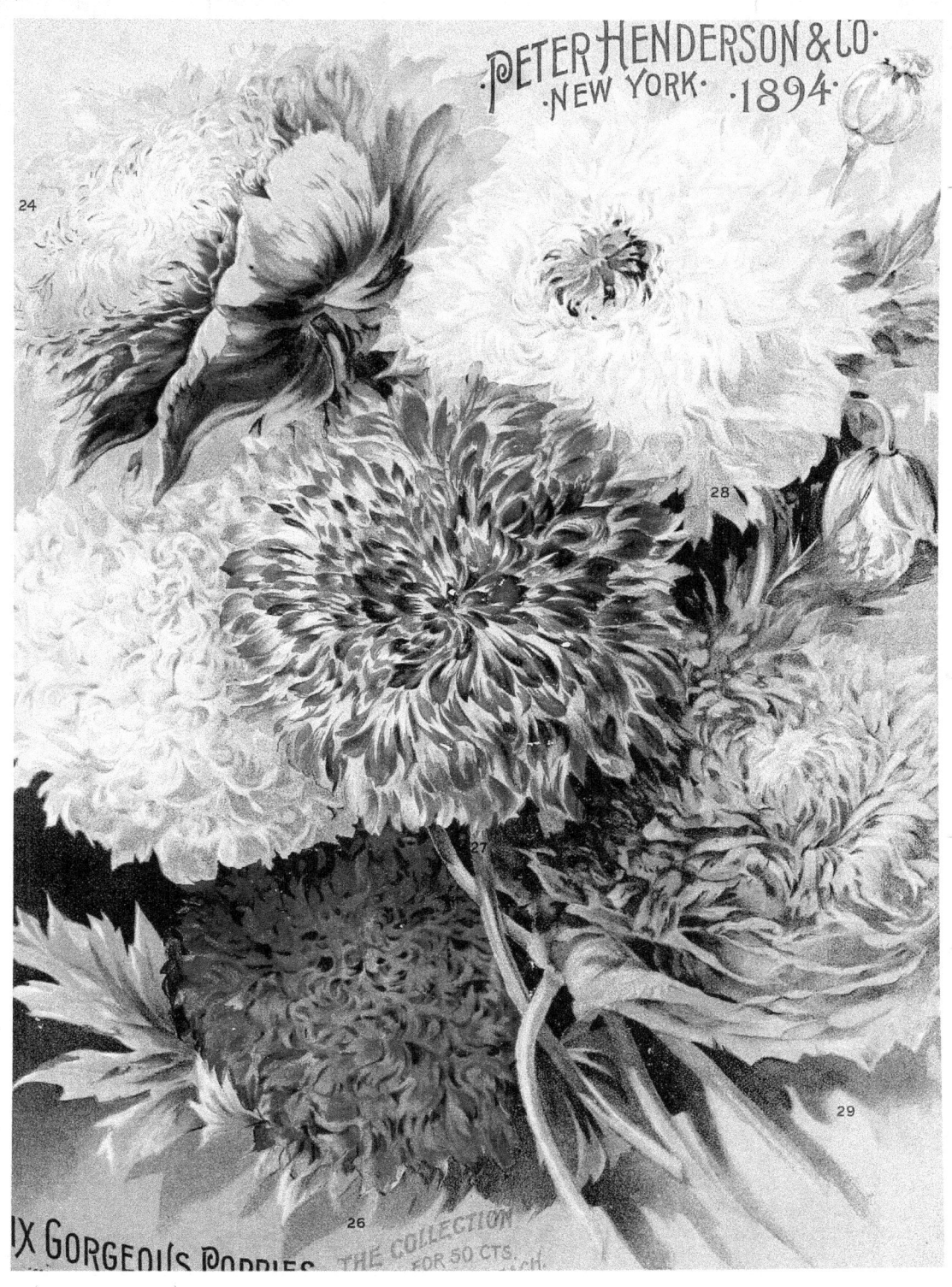

"If I had a single flower for every time I think about you, I could walk forever in my garden." ~ Claudia Adrienne Grandi

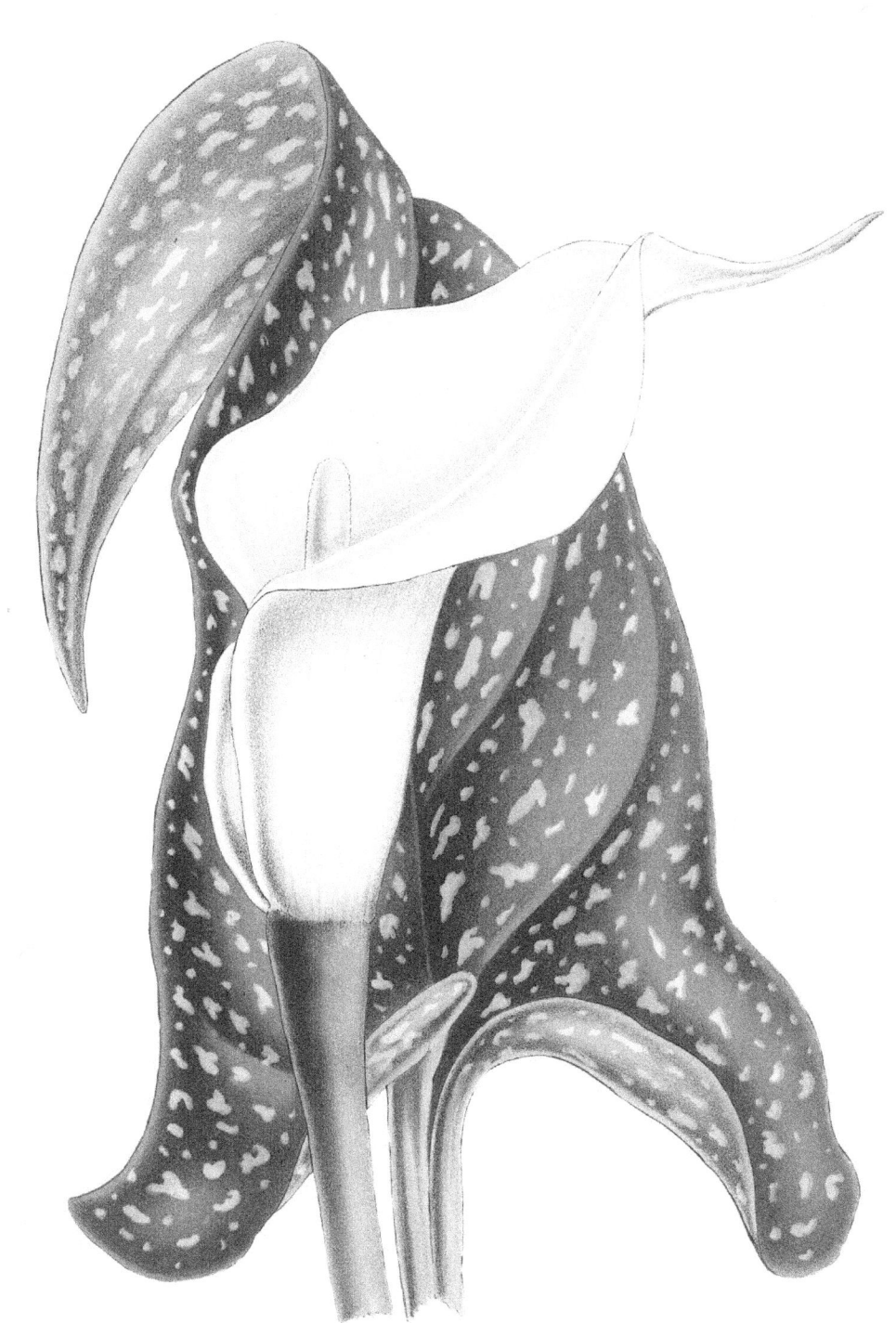

"A flower cannot blossom without sunshine, and man cannot live without love."
~ Max Muller

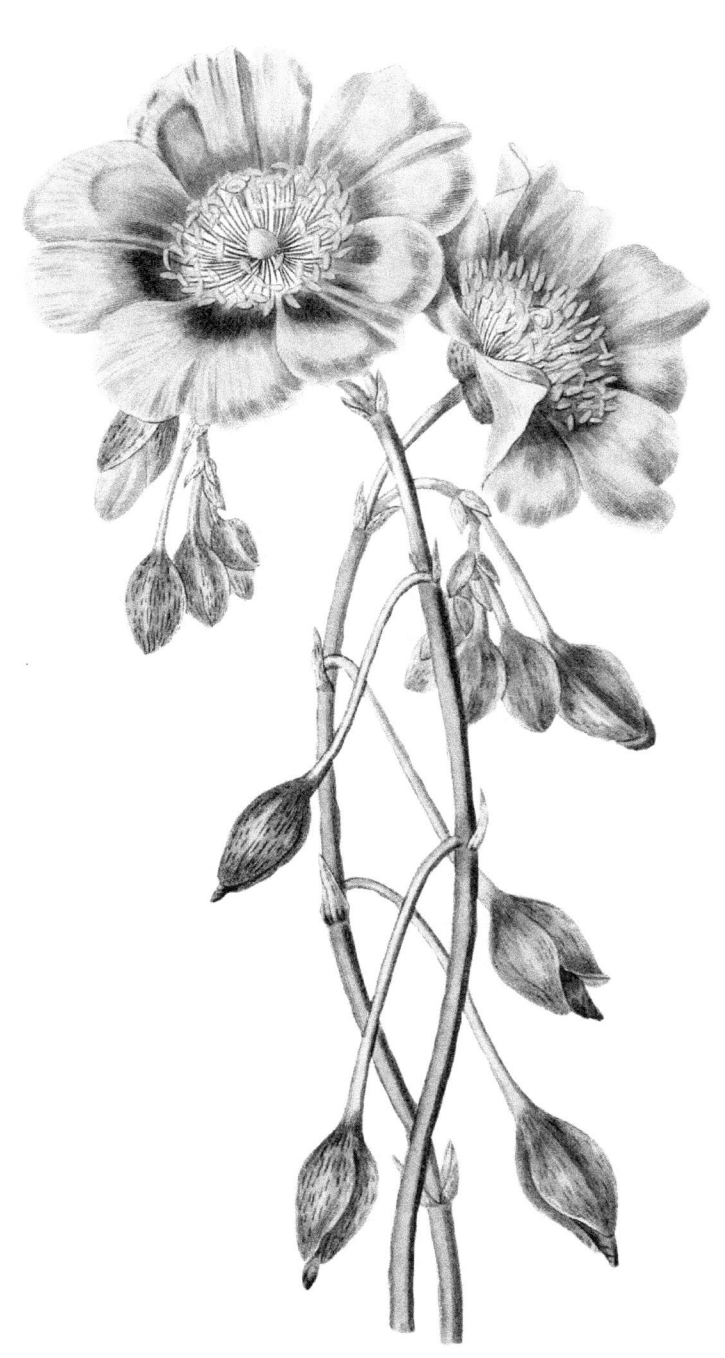

"Love is like a beautiful flower which I may not touch, but whose fragrance makes the garden a place of delight just the same."
~ Helen Keller

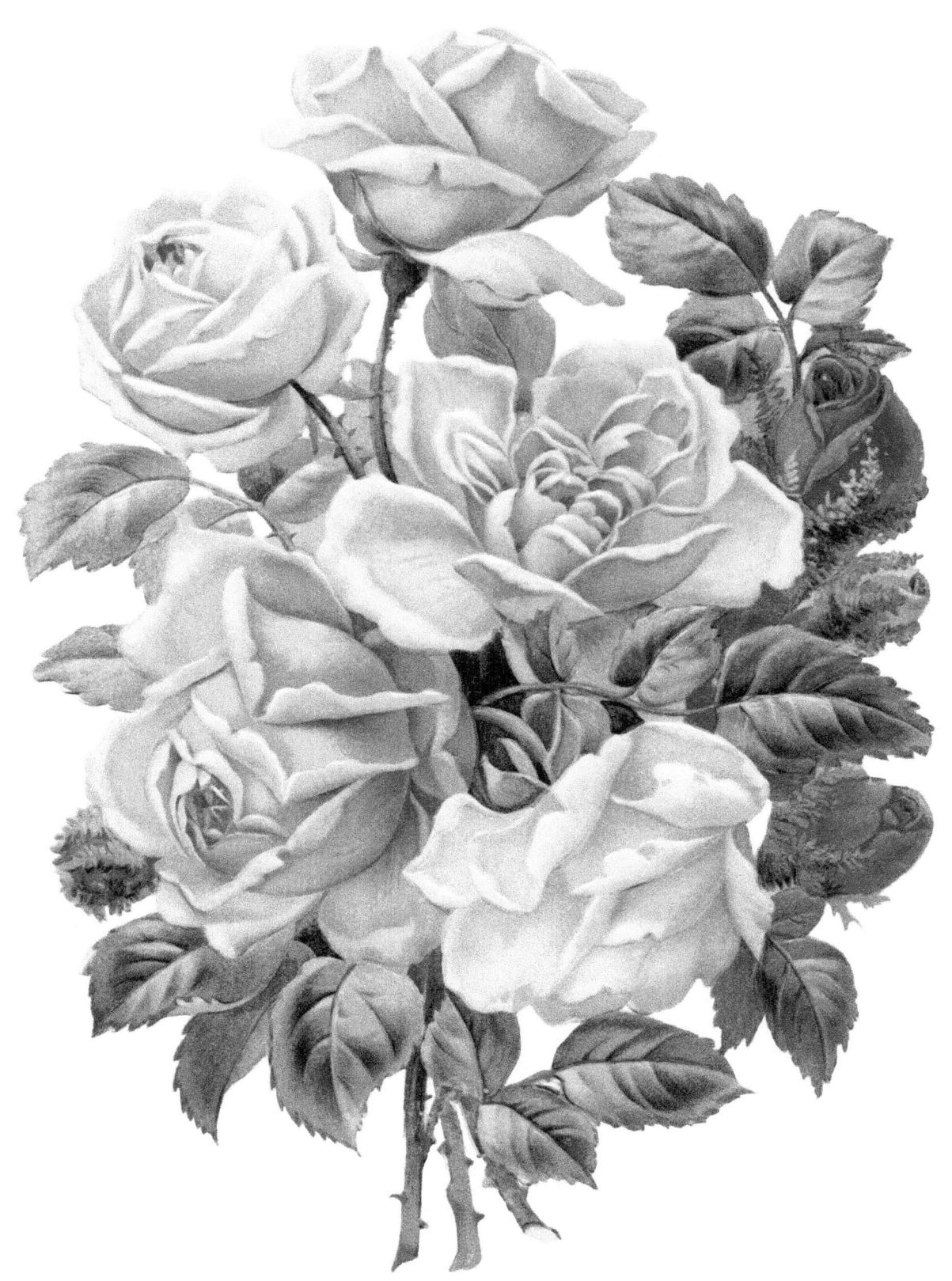

"Love is the flower you've
got to let grow."
~ John Lennon

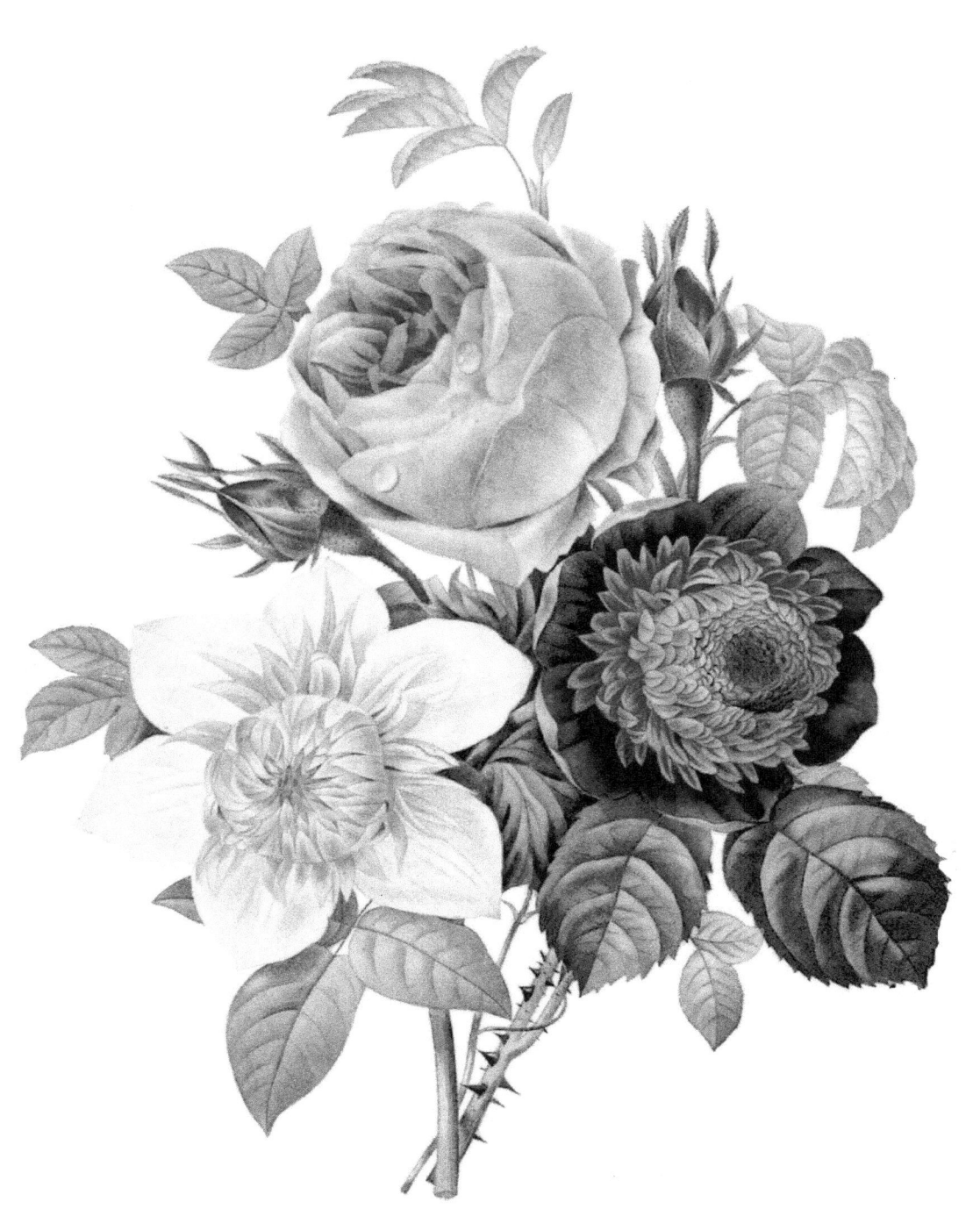

"Flowers are the music of the ground. From earth's lips spoken without sound." ~ Edwin Curran

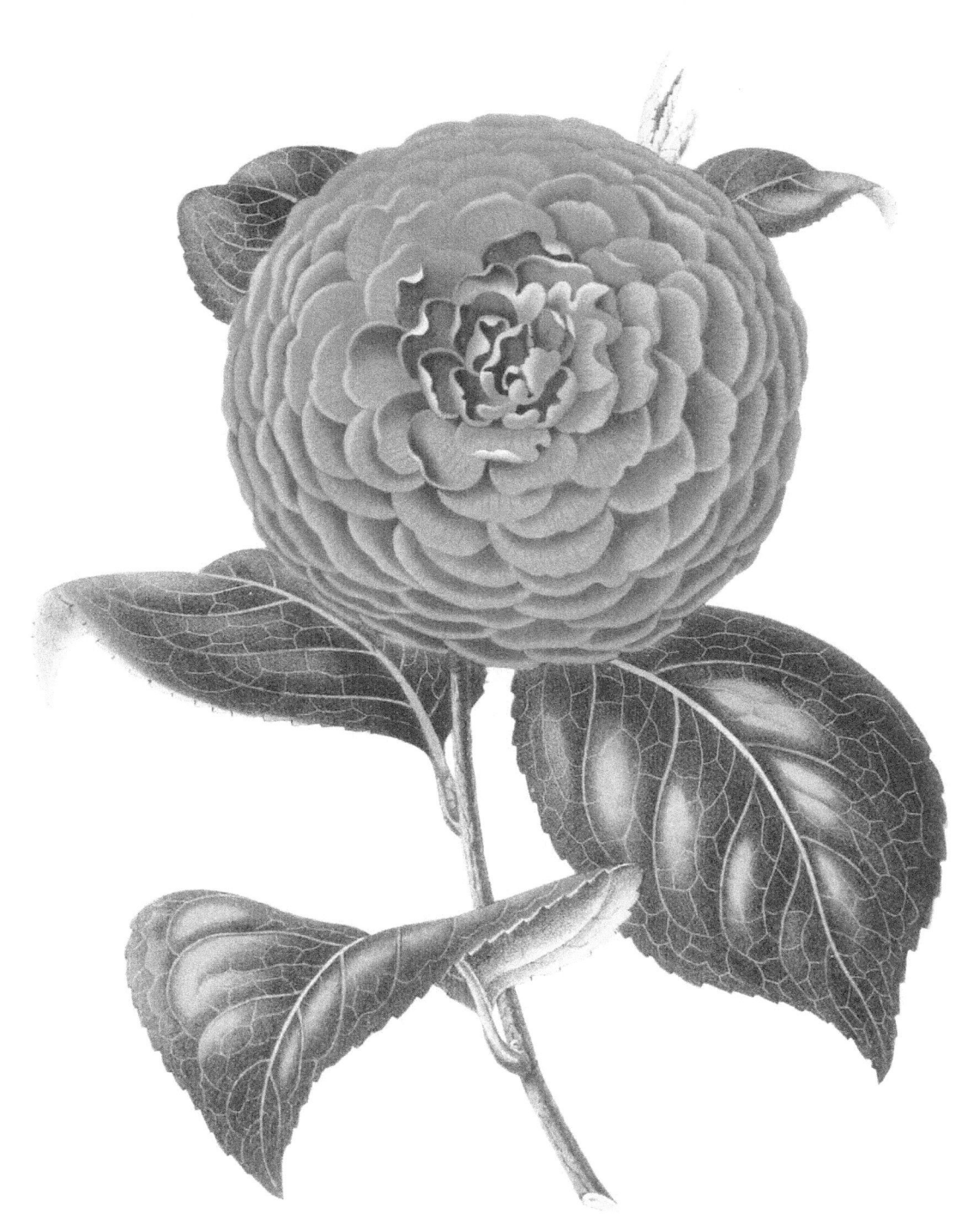

"Flowers don't worry about how they're going to bloom. They just open up and turn toward the light and that makes them beautiful."
~ Jim Carrey

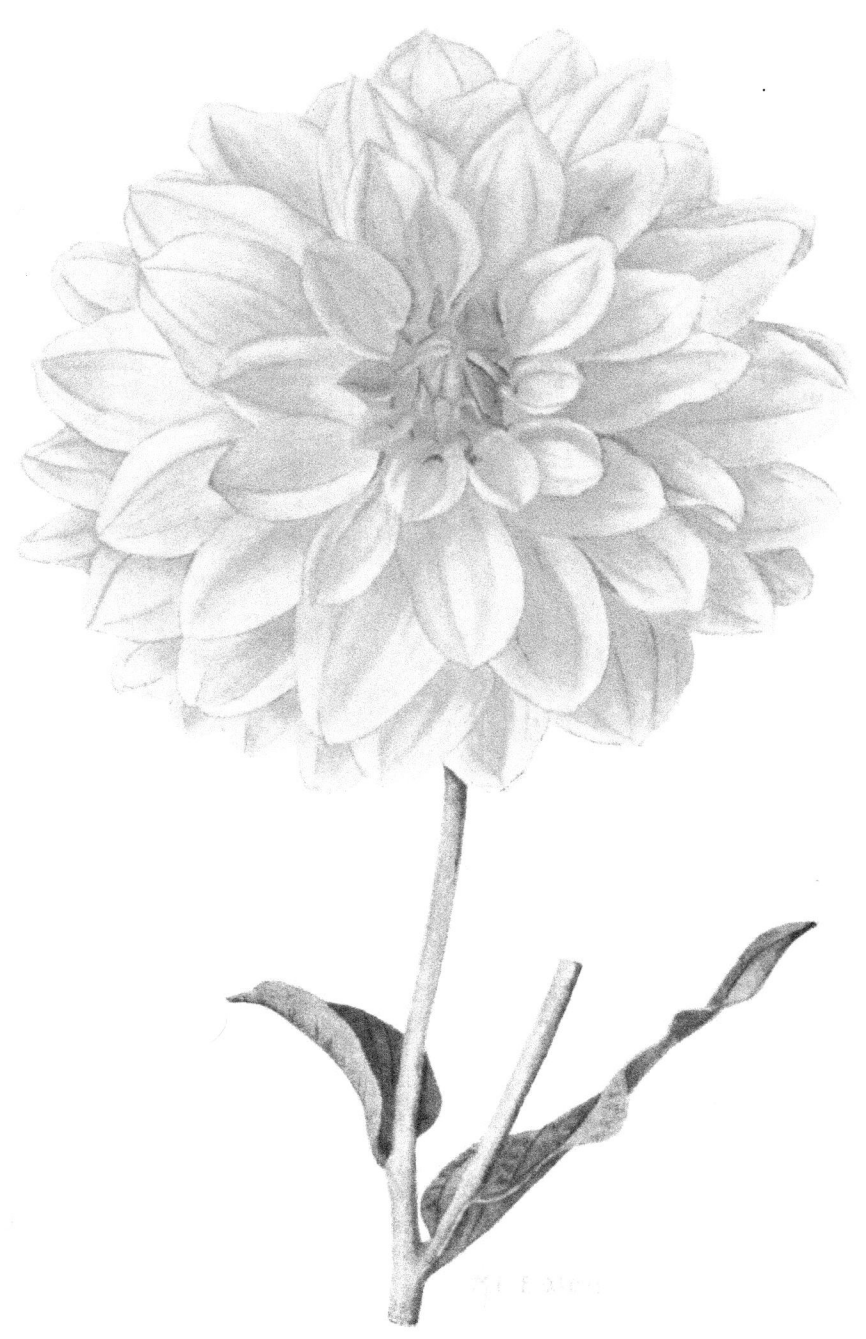

DAHLIA "KING OF THE AUTUMN"

*"All the flowers of the tomorrows
are in the seeds of today."
~ Indian Proverb*

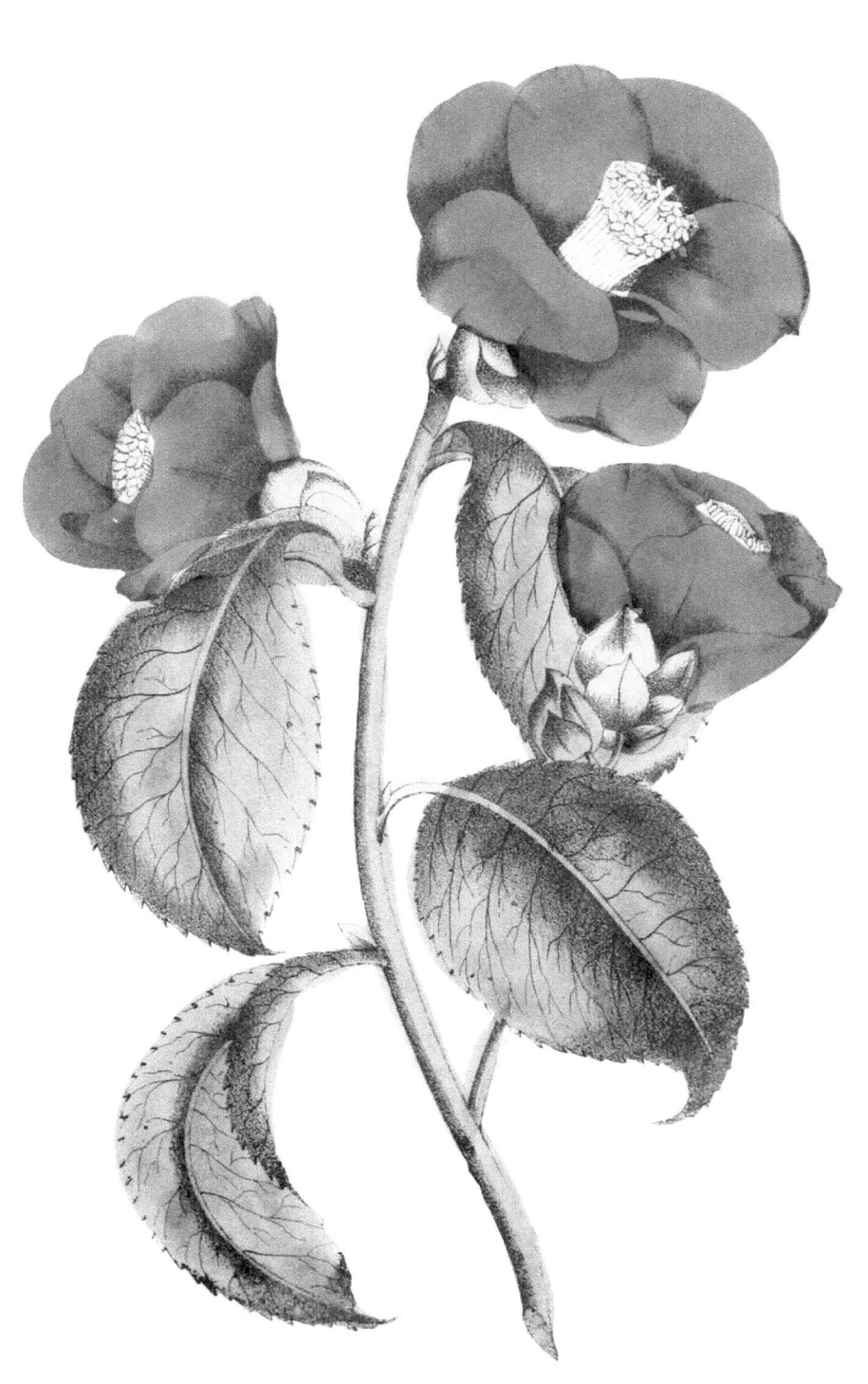

"Where flowers bloom so does hope." ~ Lady Bird Johnson

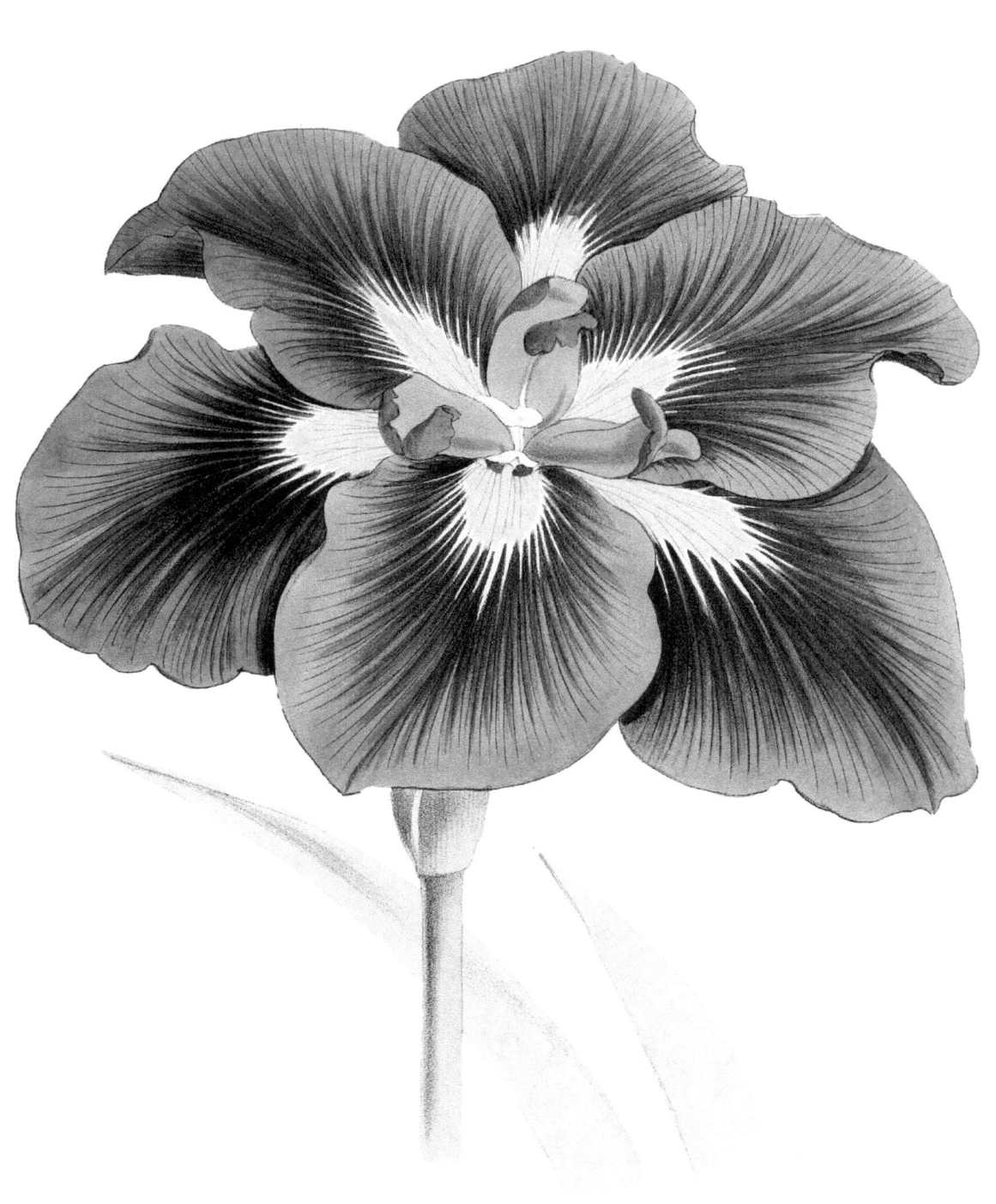

"Flowers are the hieroglyphics of angels, loved by all men for the beauty of their character, though few can decipher even fragments of their meaning."
~ Lydia M. Child

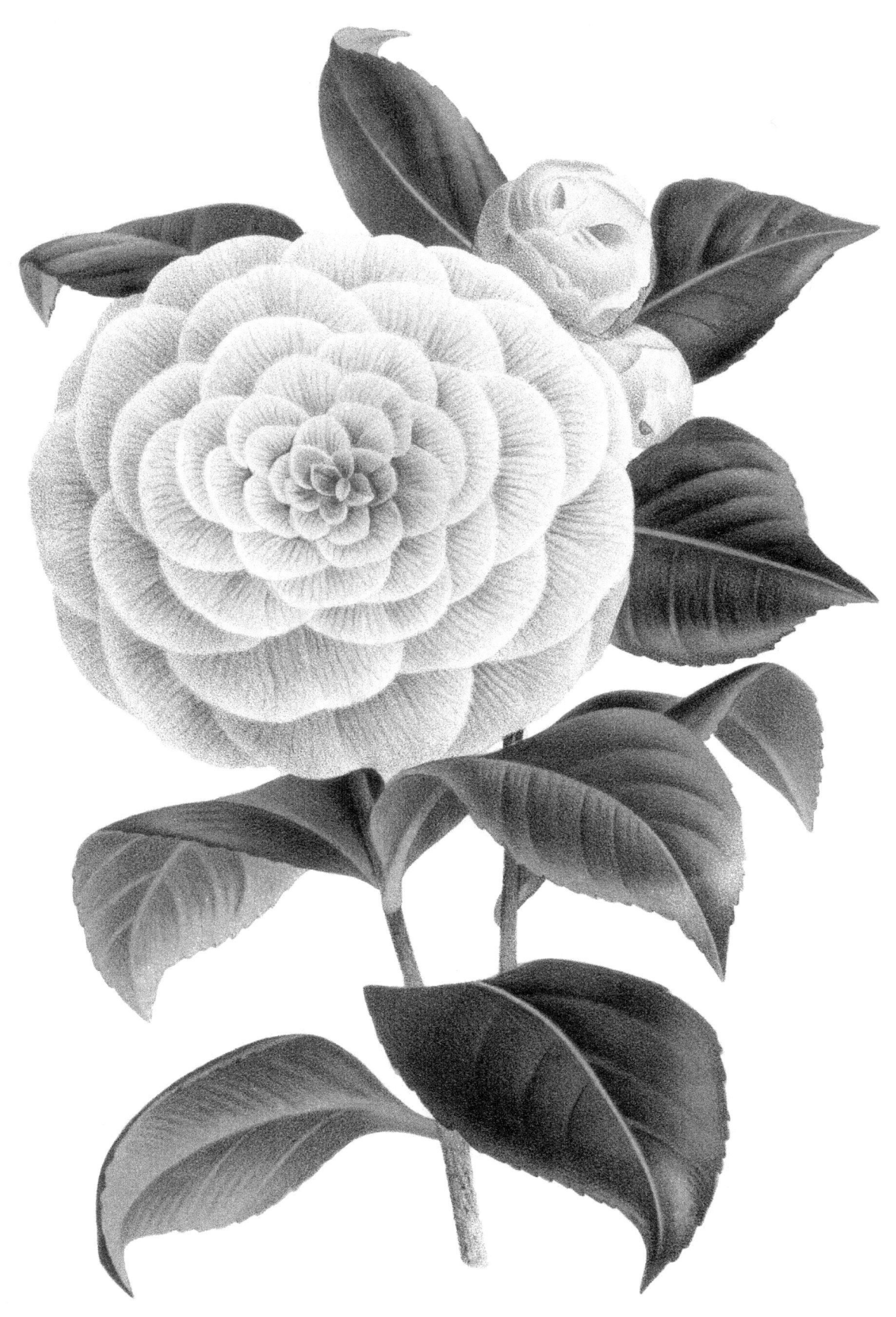

"Flowers always make people better, happier and more helpful; they are sunshine, food and medicine to the soul."
~ Luther Burbank

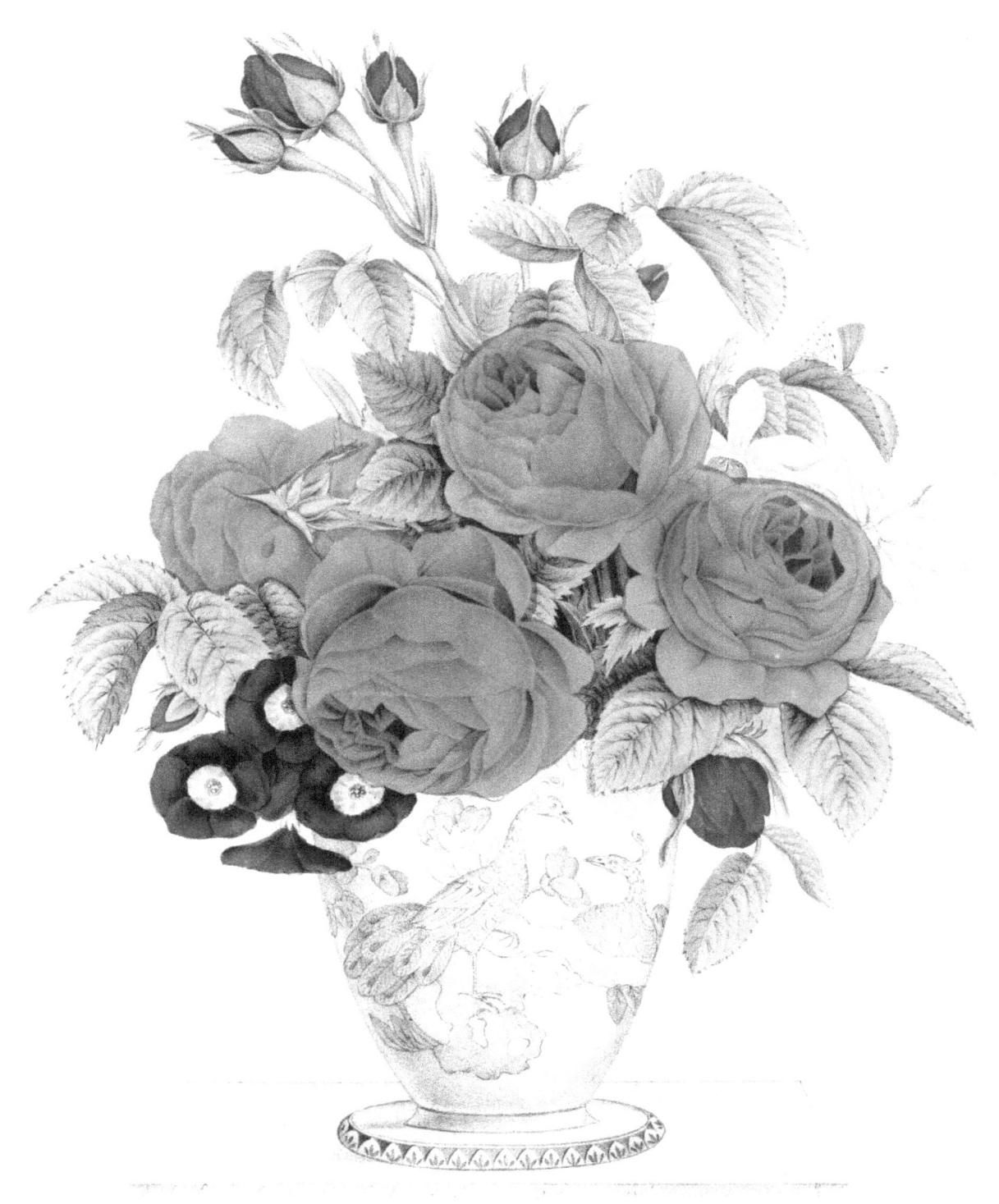

THE BOQUET.

"Flowers are the sweetest things God ever made, and forgot to put a soul into."
~ Henry Beecher

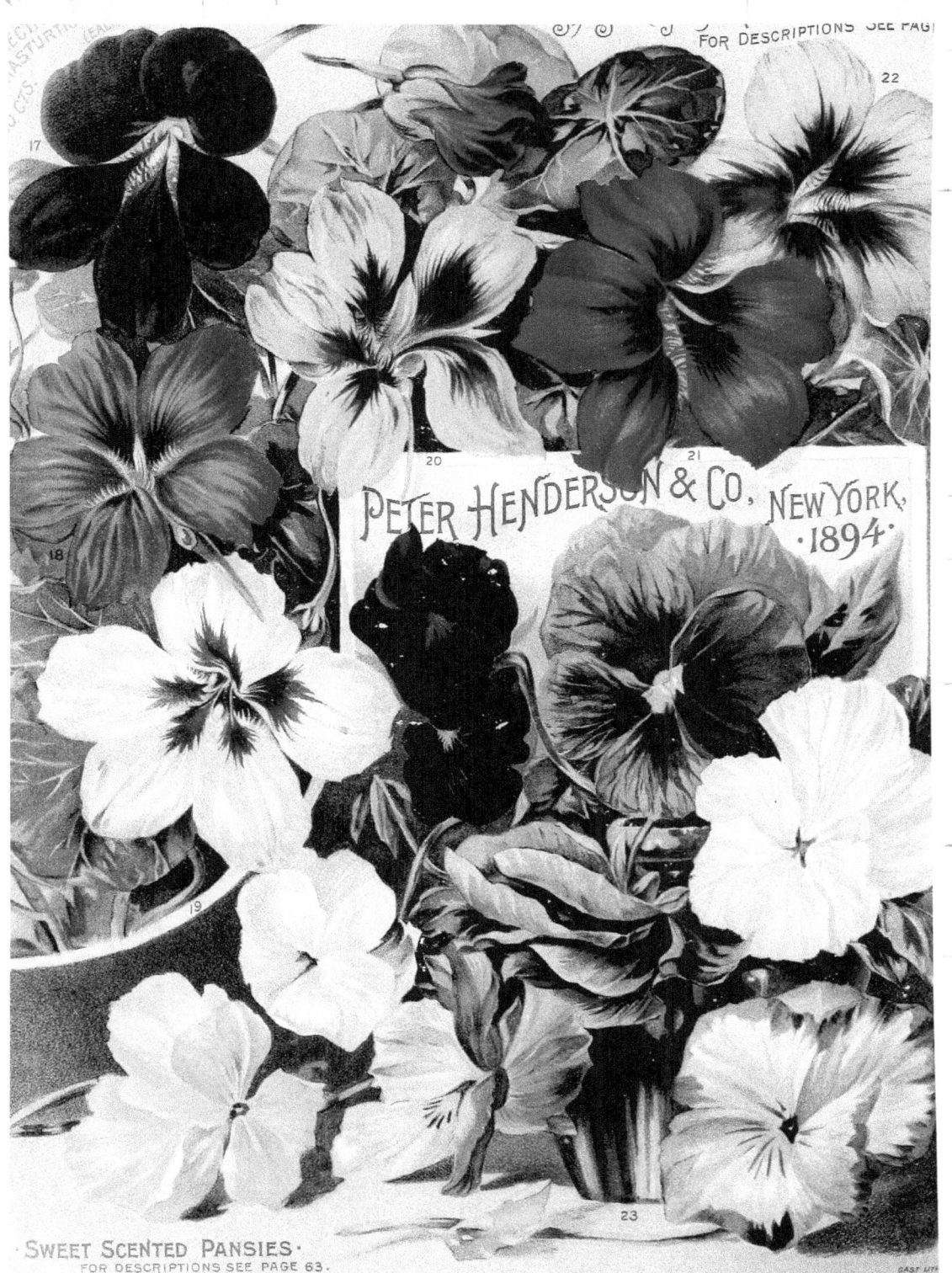

"Flowers are those little colorful beacons of the sun from which we get sunshine when dark, somber skies blanket our thoughts."
~ Dodinsky

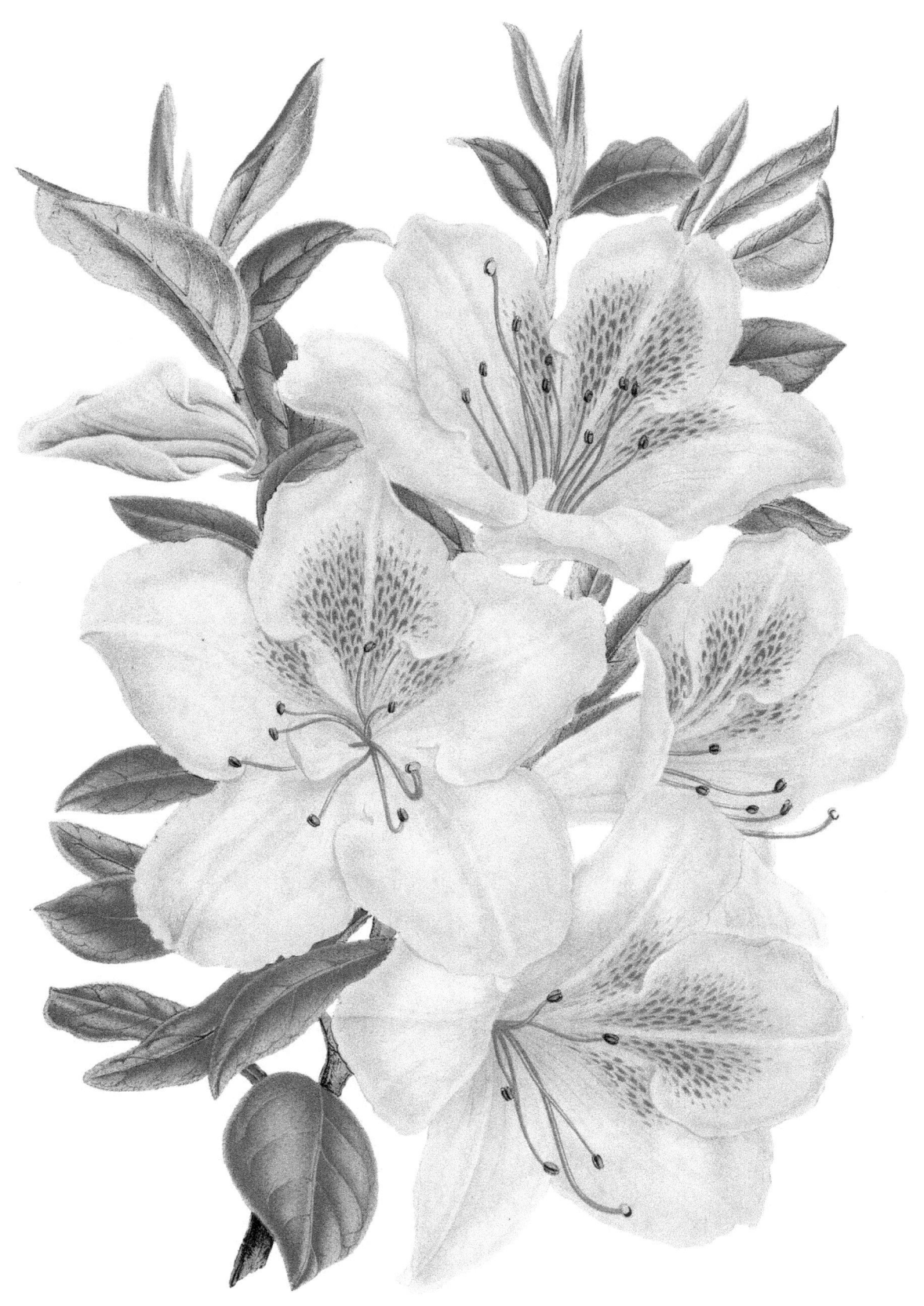

"Earth laughs in flowers."
~ Ralph Waldo Emerson,
"Hamatreya"

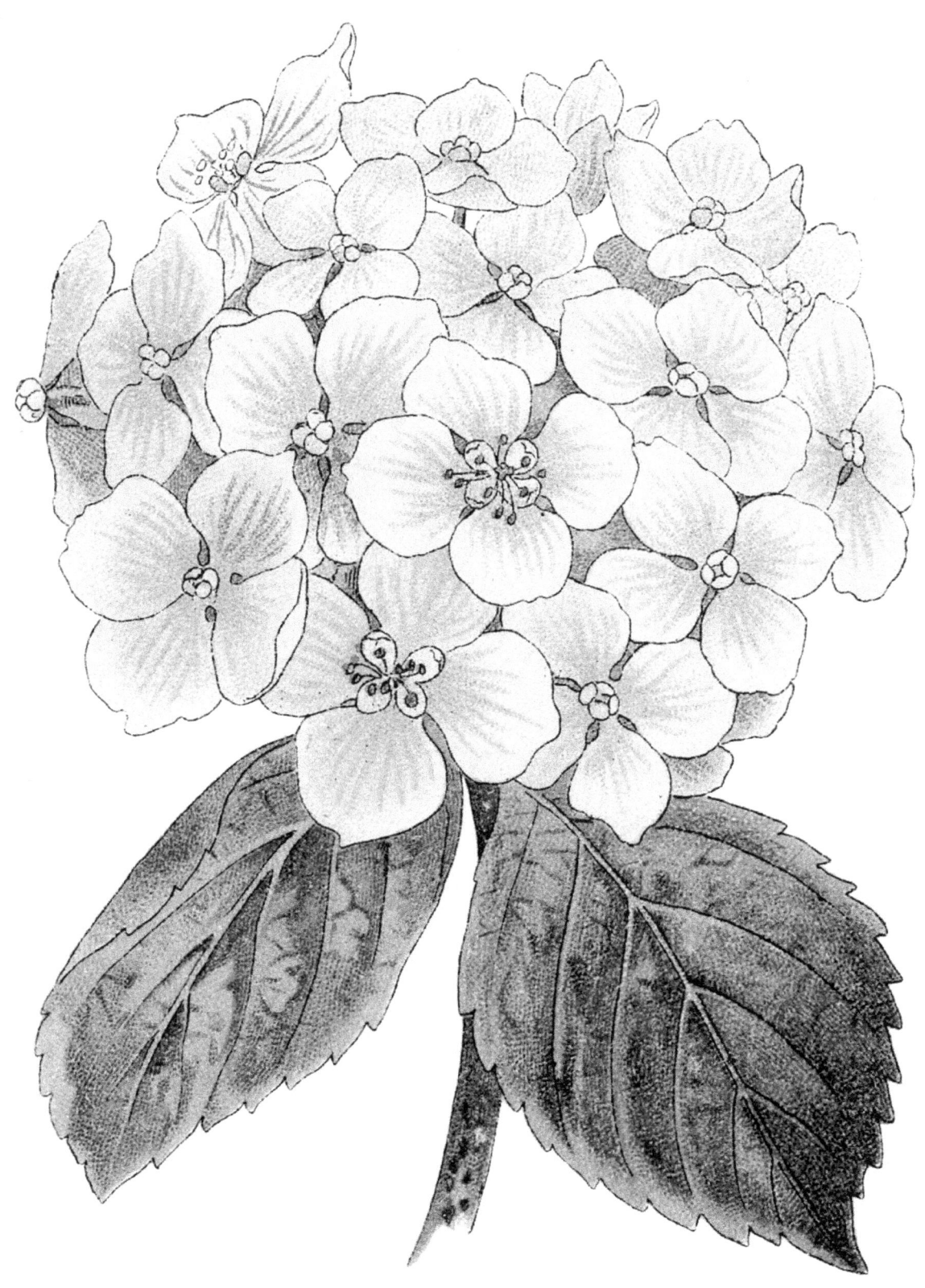

"To be overcome by the fragrance of flowers is a delectable form of defeat."
~ Beverly Nichols

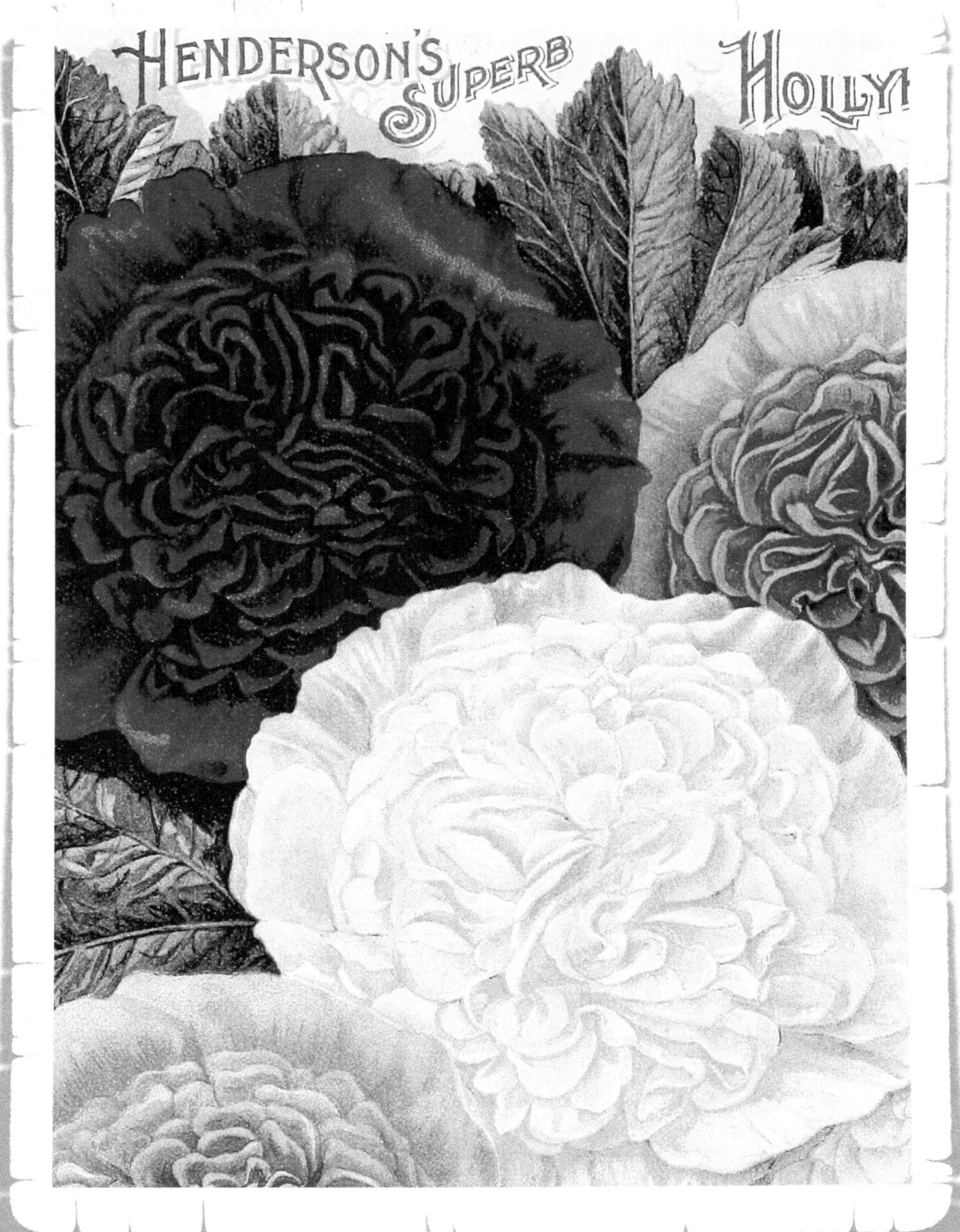

"Every flower is a soul blossoming in nature."
~ Gerard de Nerval

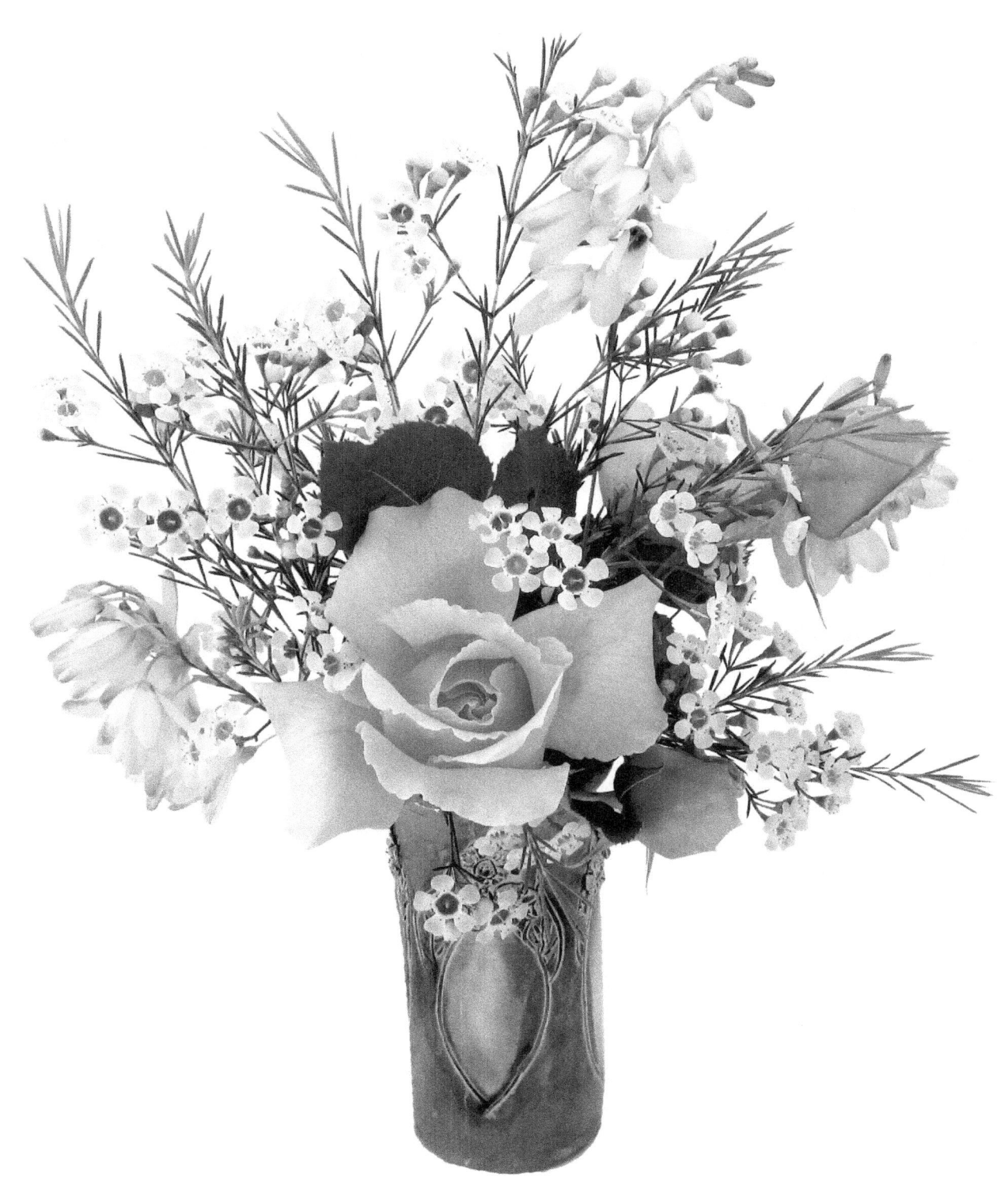

*"To see a world in a grain of sand
and heaven in a wild flower
is to hold infinity in the palm of
your hand and eternity in an hour."
~ William Blake*

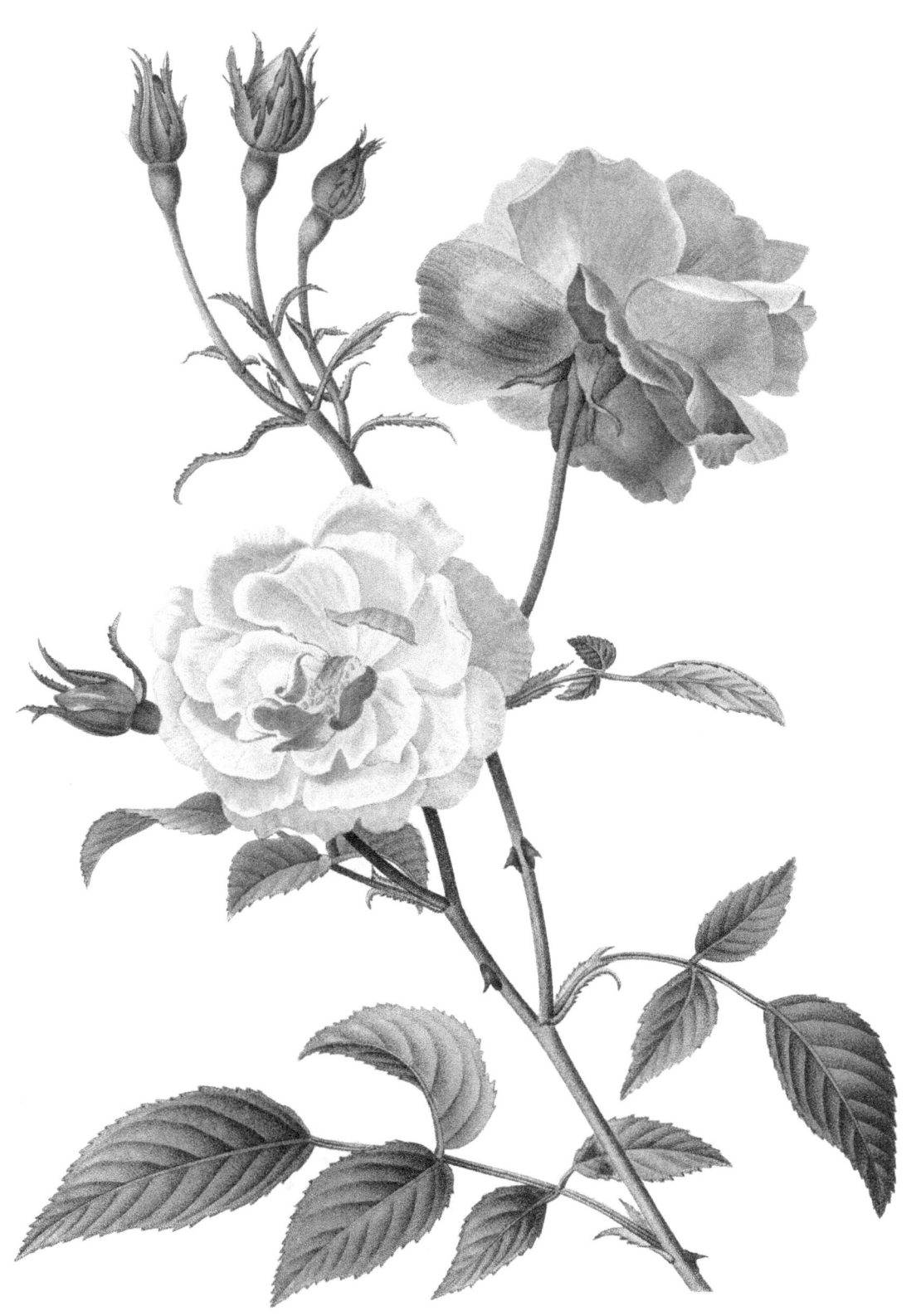

"Be honest, be nice. Be a flower not a weed."
~ Aaron Neville

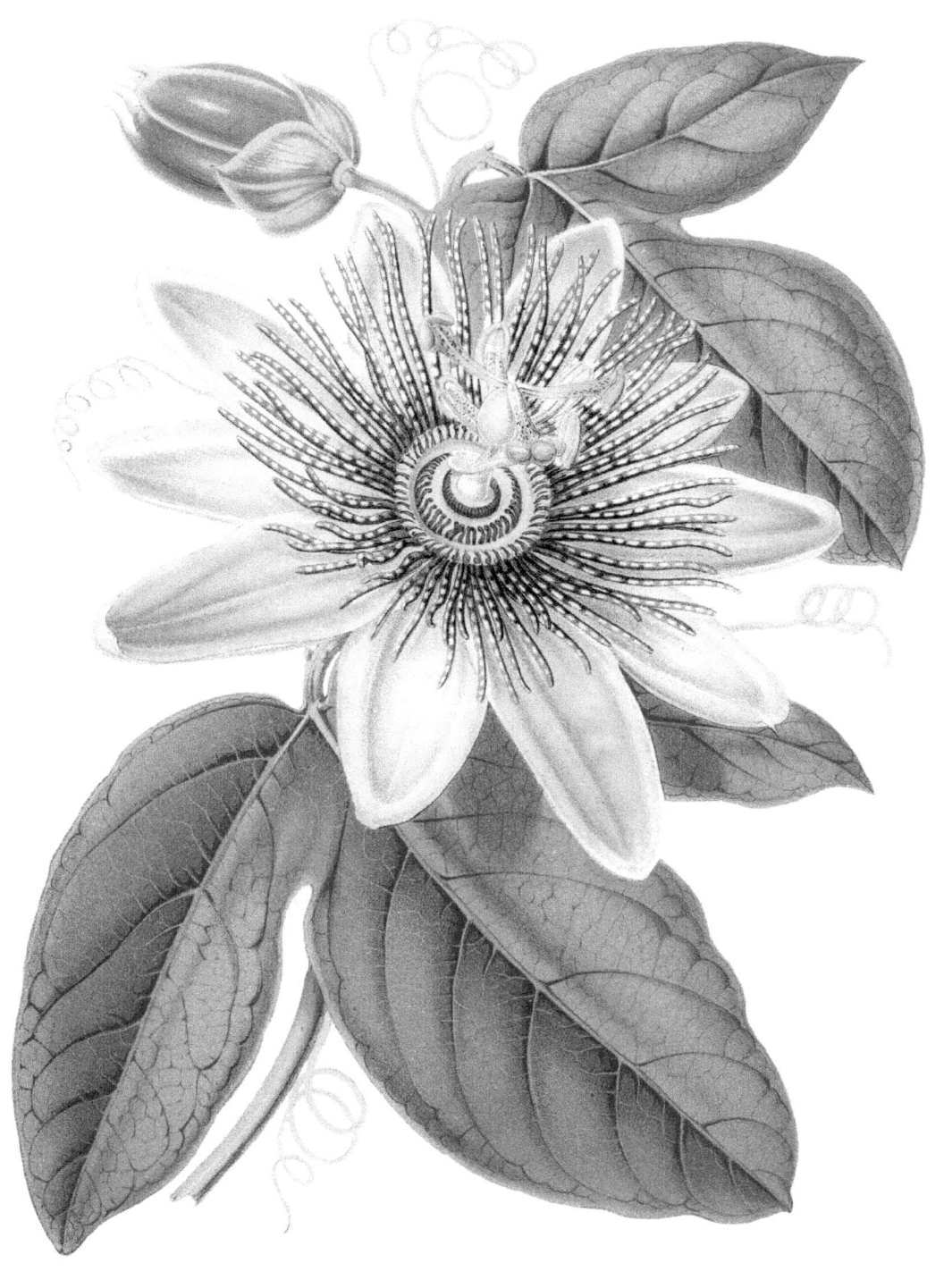

"The fairest thing in nature, a flower, still has its roots in earth and manure."
~ D. H. Lawrence

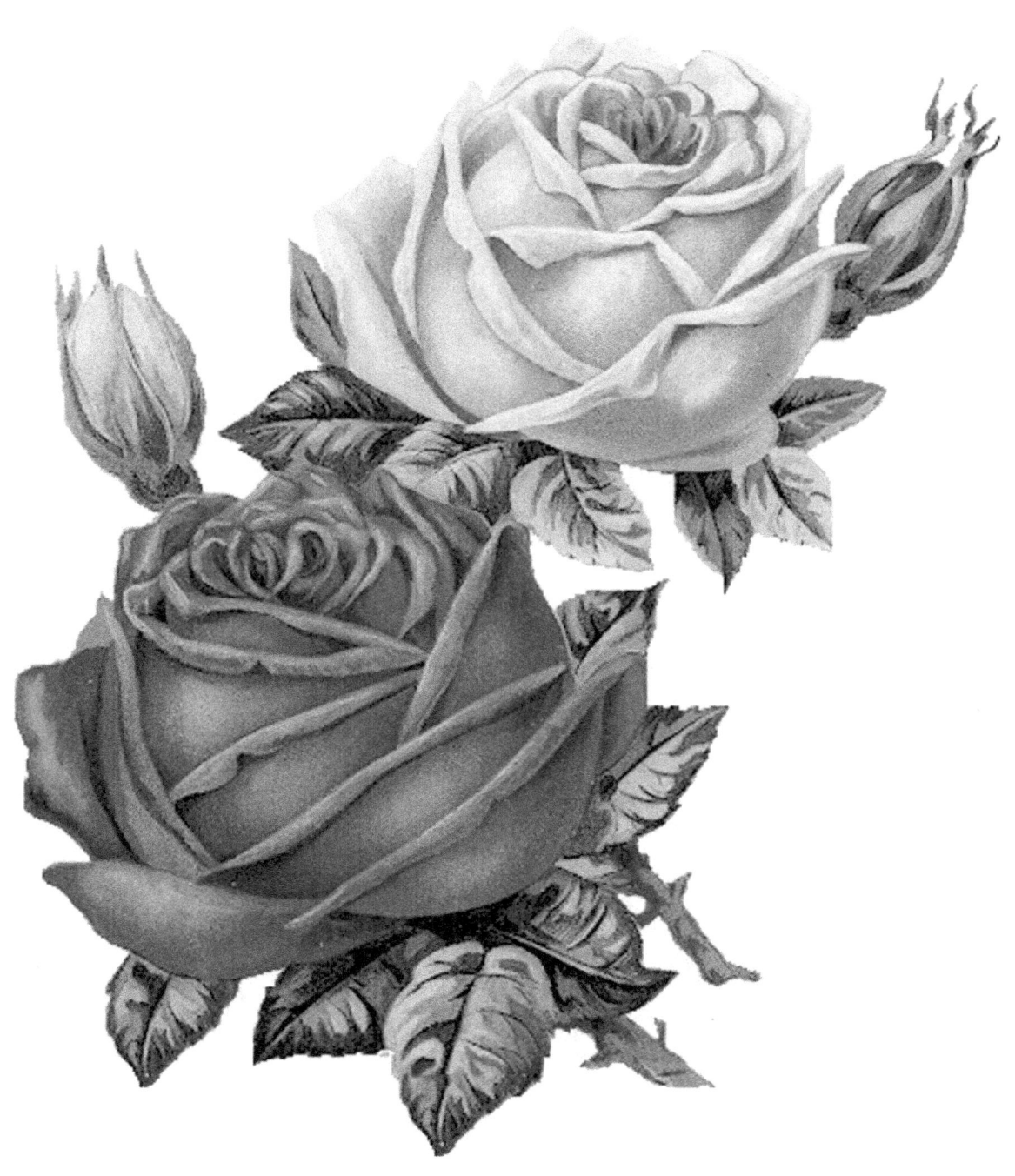

"Happiness radiates like the fragrance of a flower and draws all things to you."
~ Maharishi Mahesh Yogi

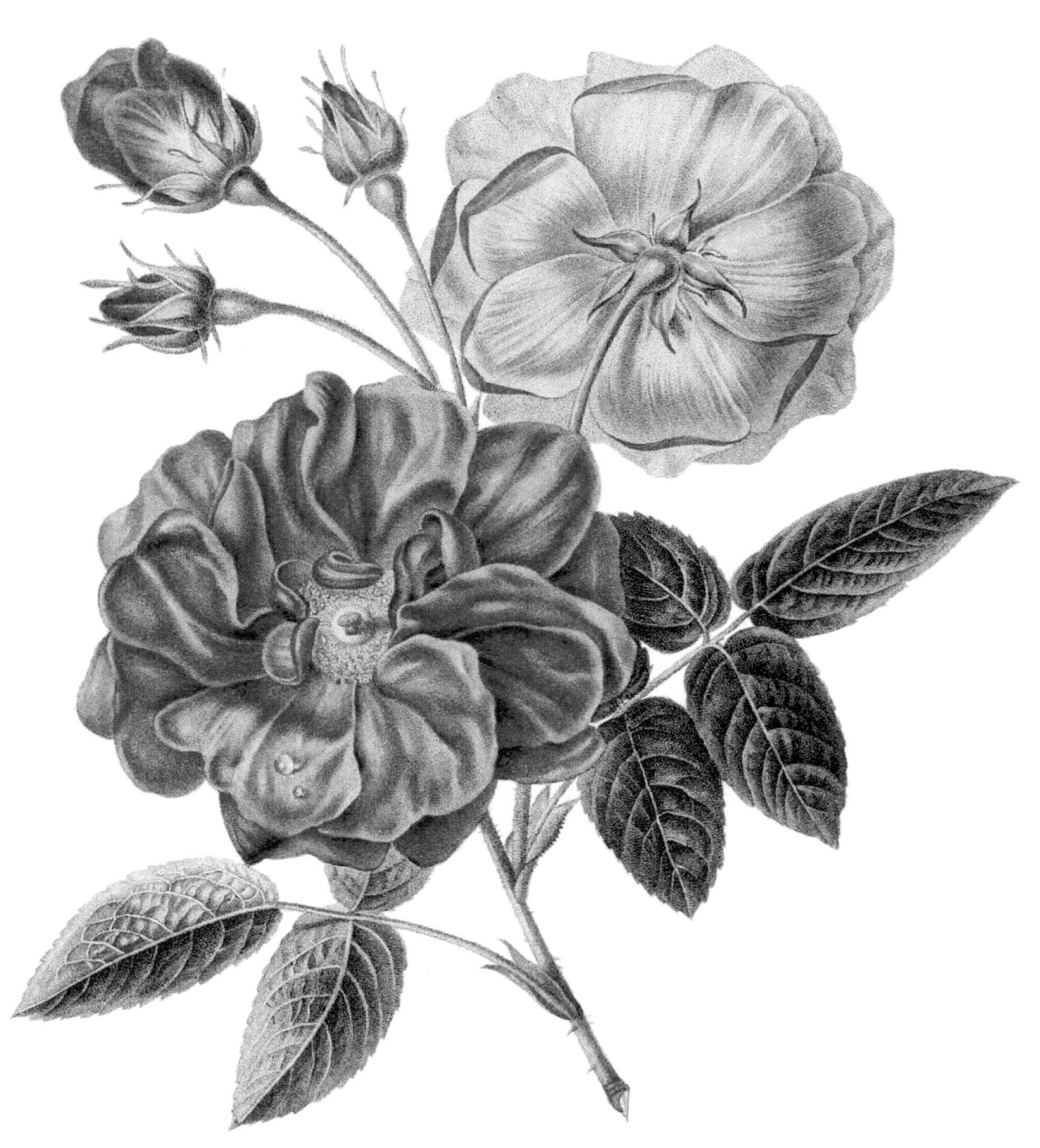

"Happiness held is the seed; happiness shared is the flower."
~ John Harrigan

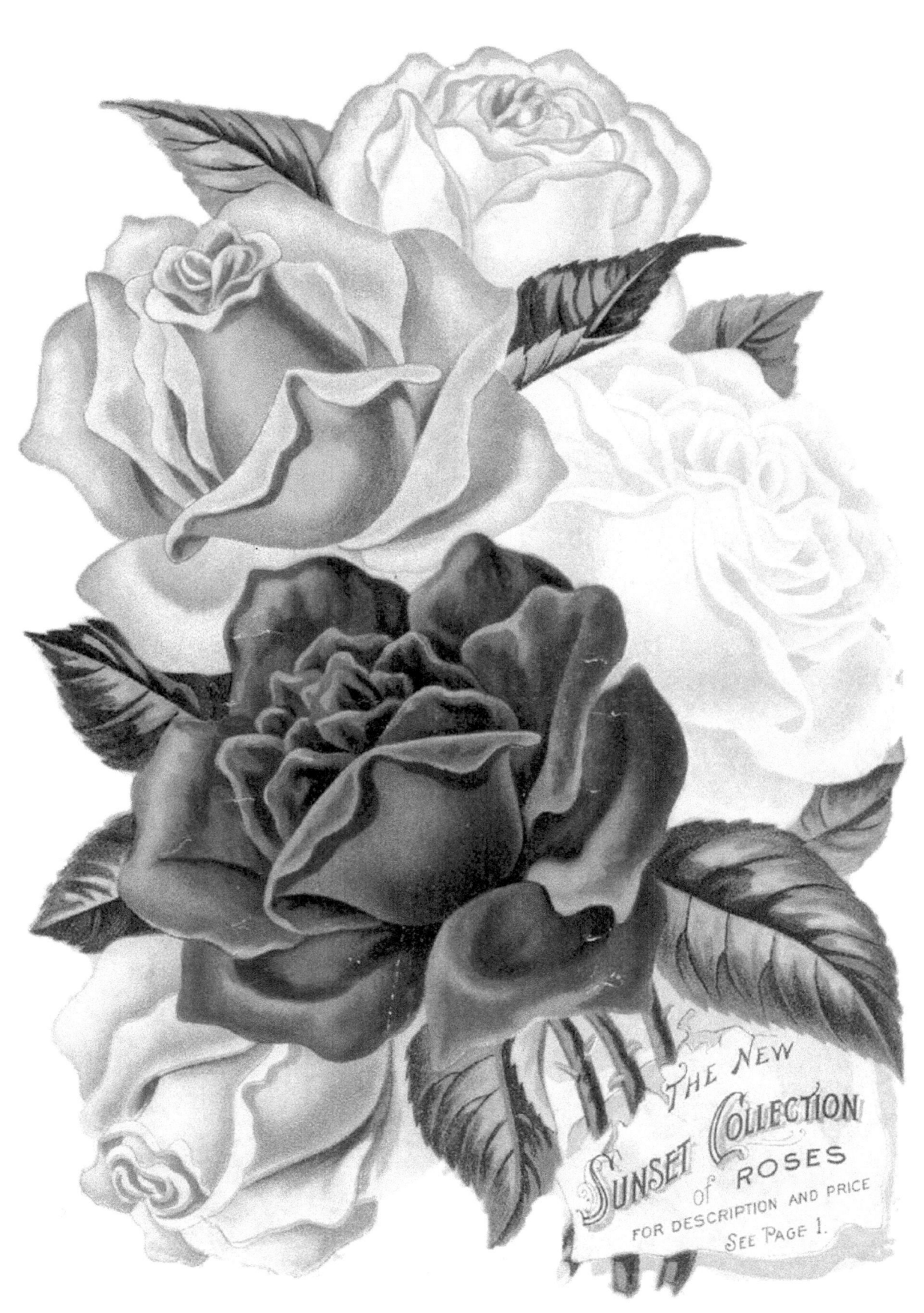

*"Love is flower like;
Friendship is like a sheltering tree."
~ Samuel Taylor Coleridge*

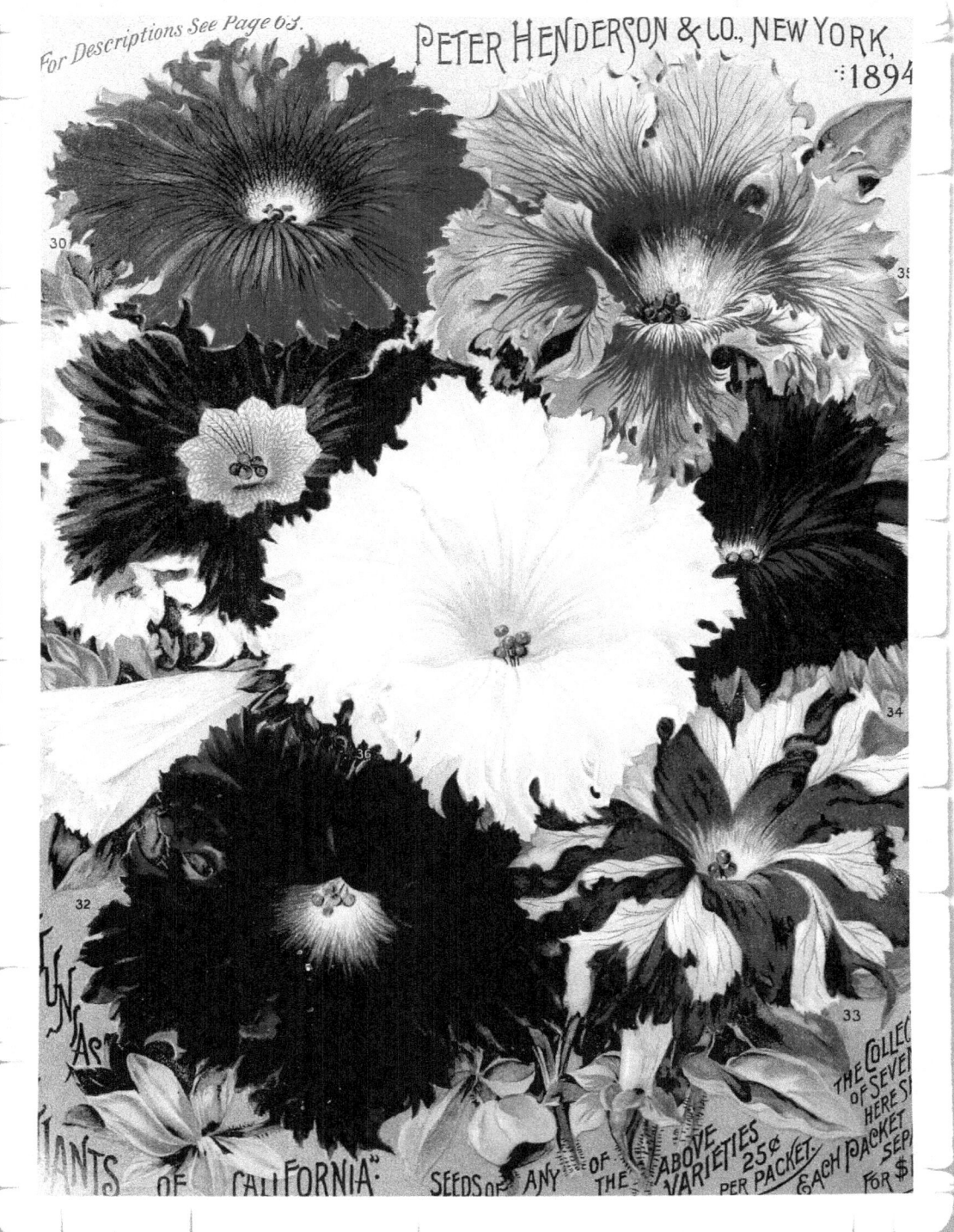

*"When you take a flower in your
hand and really look at it, it's your world
for a moment. I want to give that world
to someone else."*
~ Georgia O'Keefe

"The Amen of nature is always a flower."
~ Oliver Wendell Holmes, Sr.

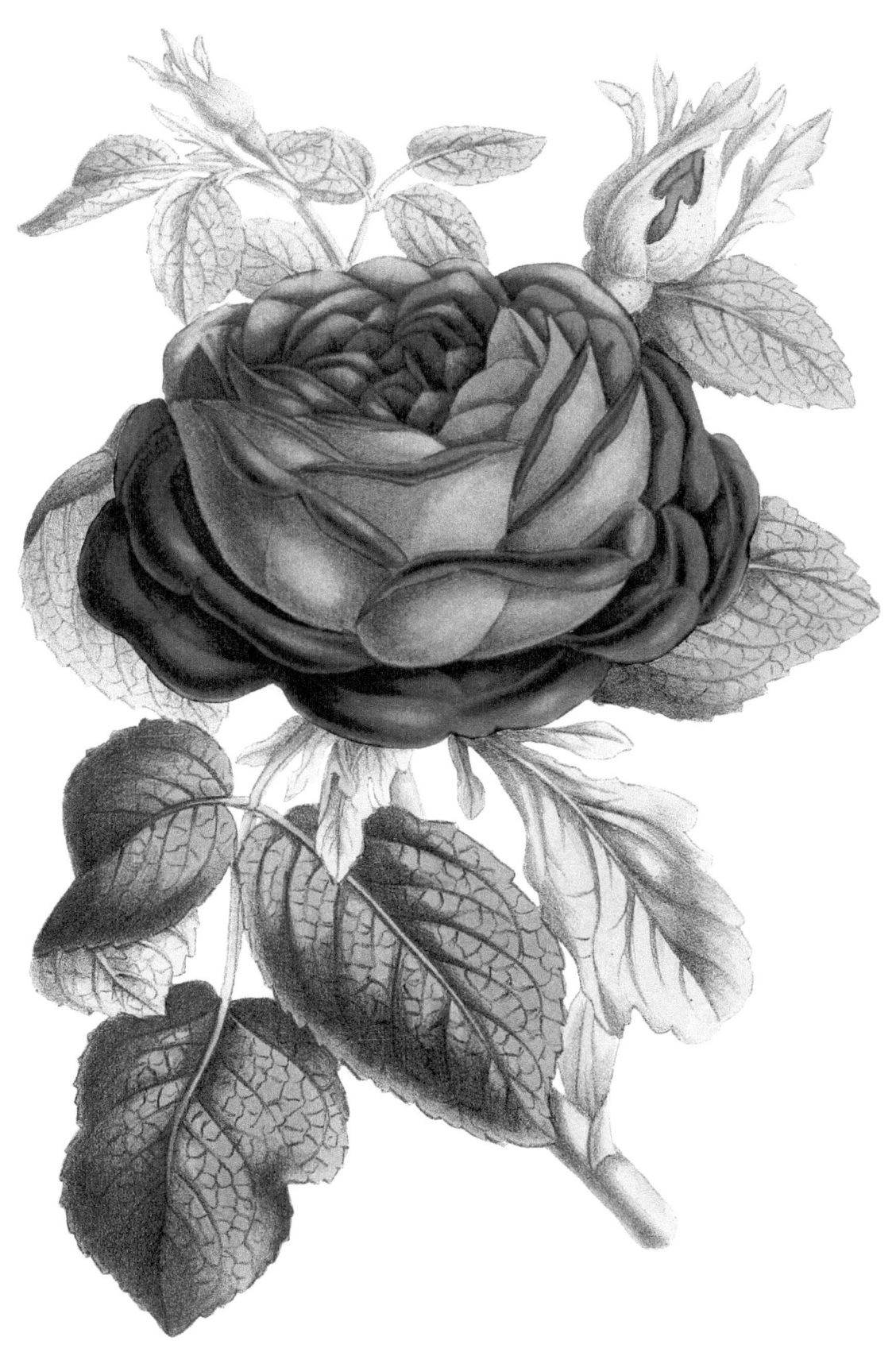

"I want it said of me by those who knew me best, that I always plucked a thistle and planted a flower where I thought a flower would grow."
~ Abraham Lincoln

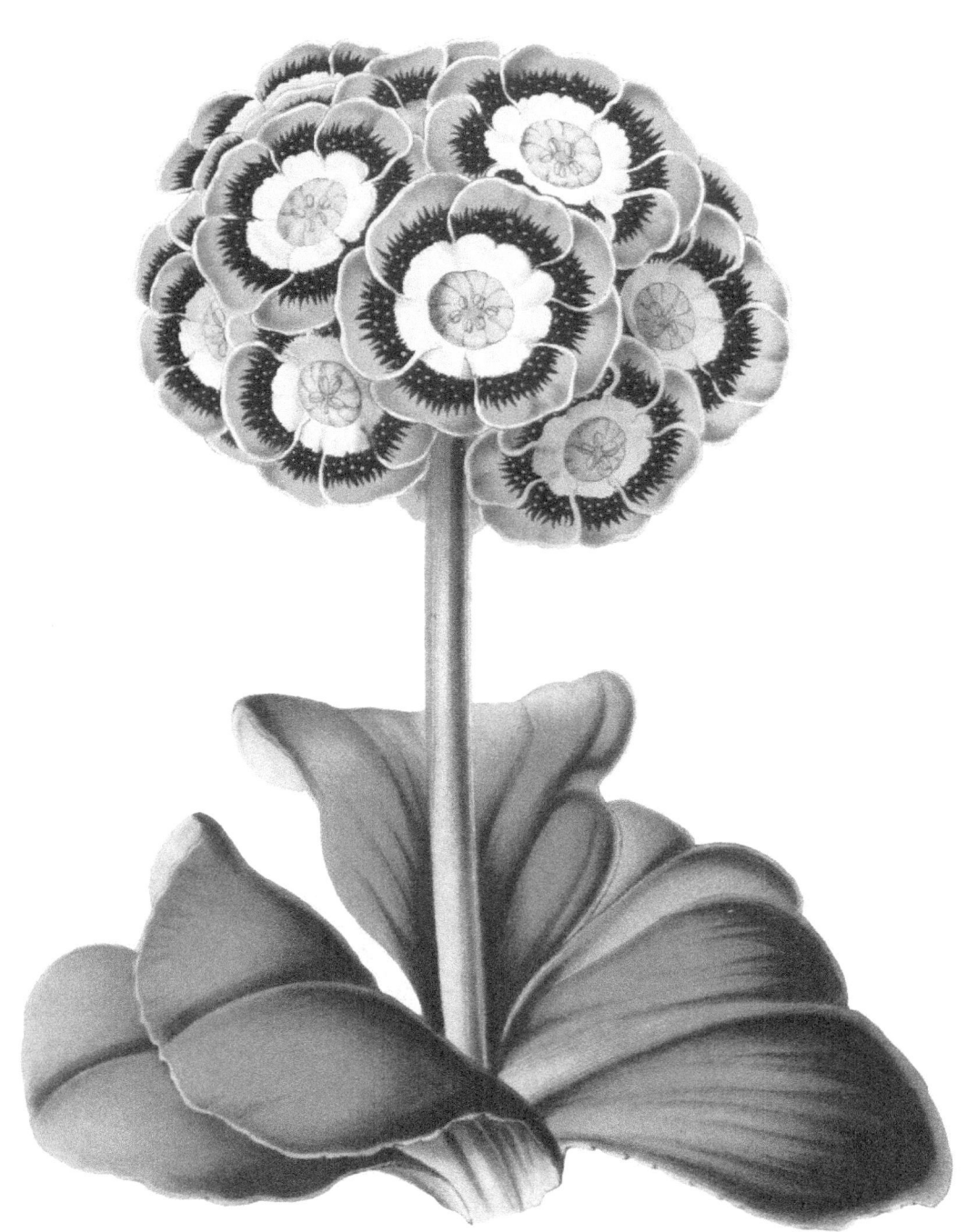

"Everything has beauty, but not everyone sees it."
~ Confucious

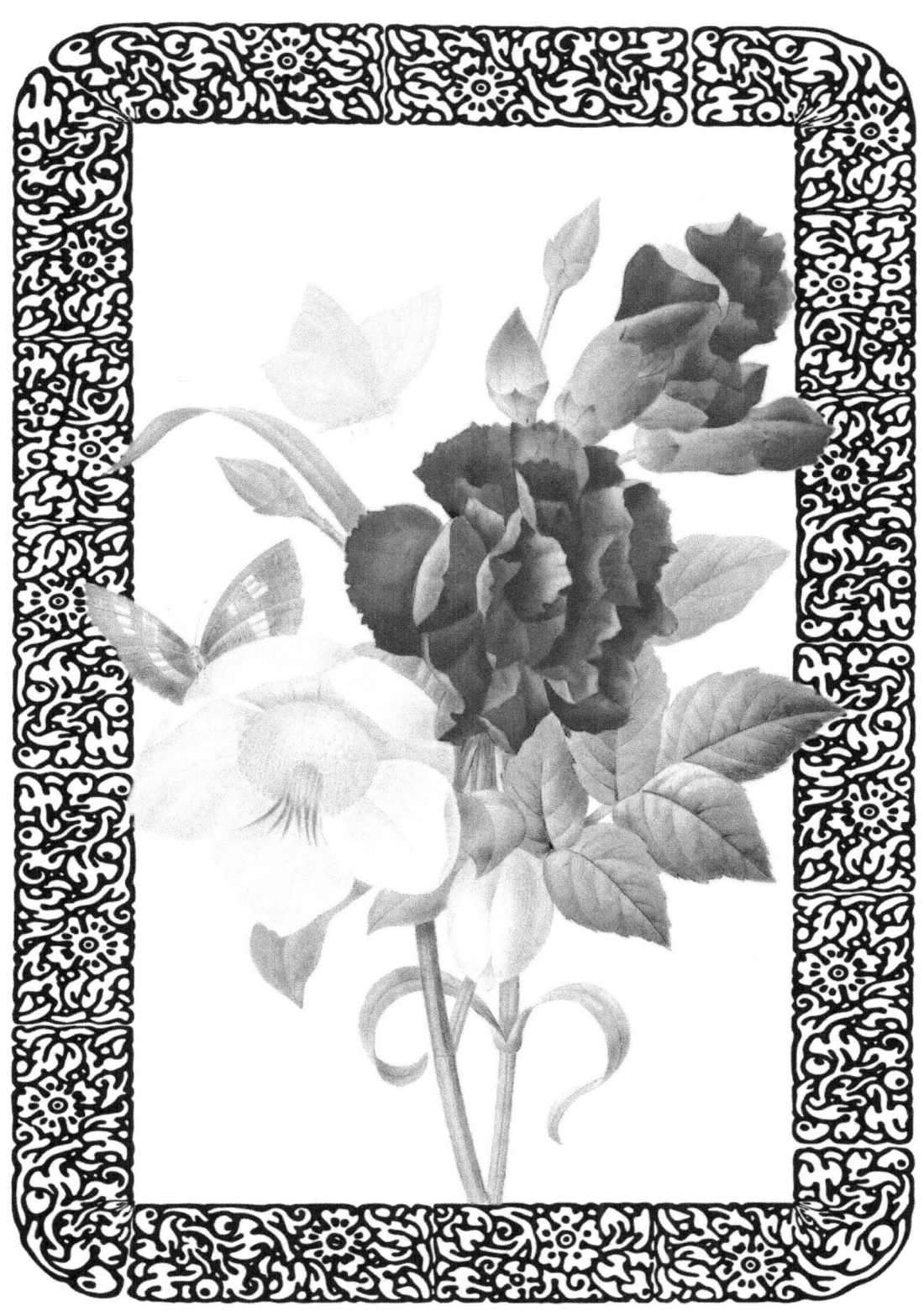

"The intoxicating fragrance of flowers are angel wings gently carrying you though heavenly gardens."
Illyssa

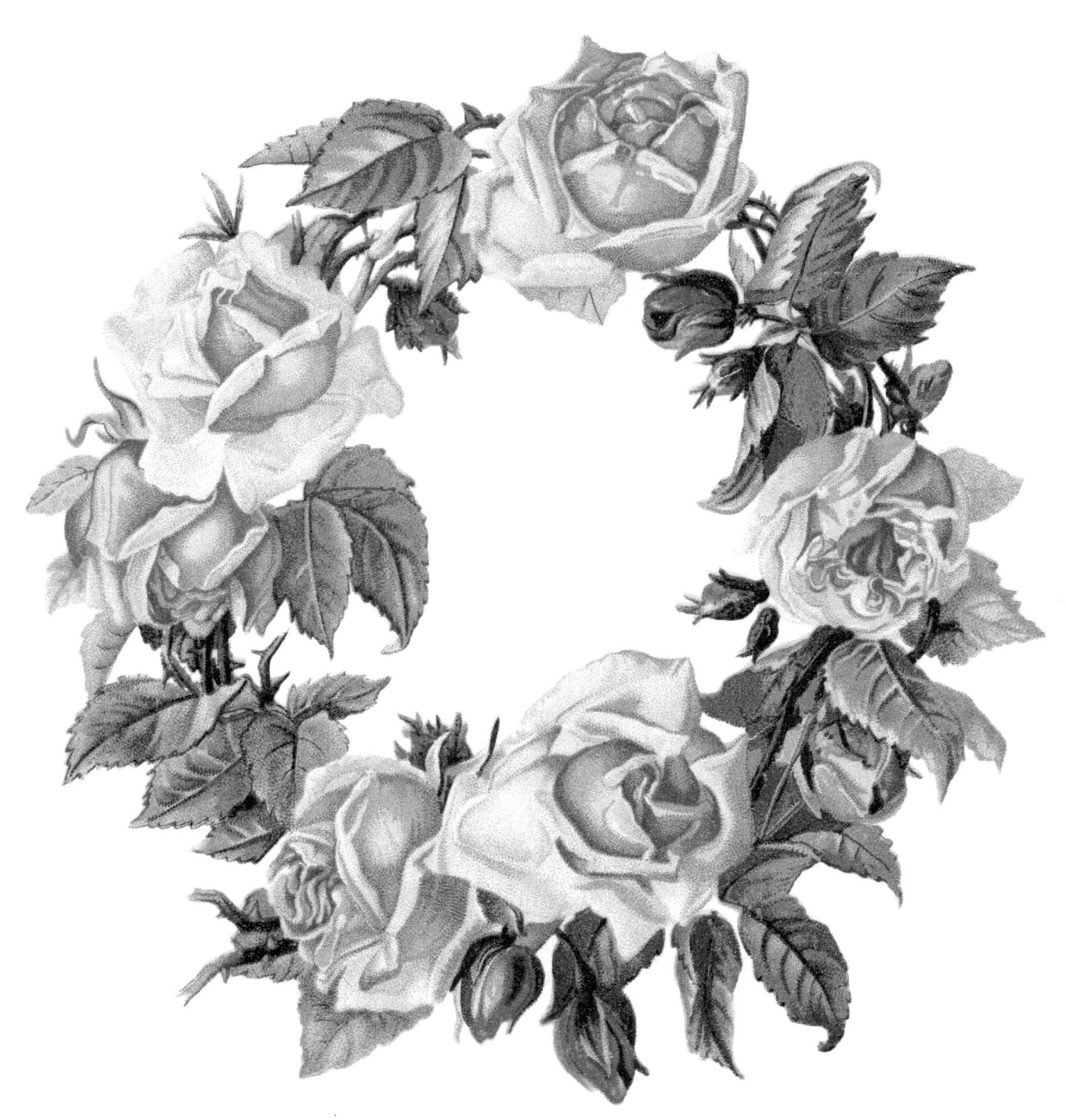

"A flower is a smile from heaven."
~ Unknown

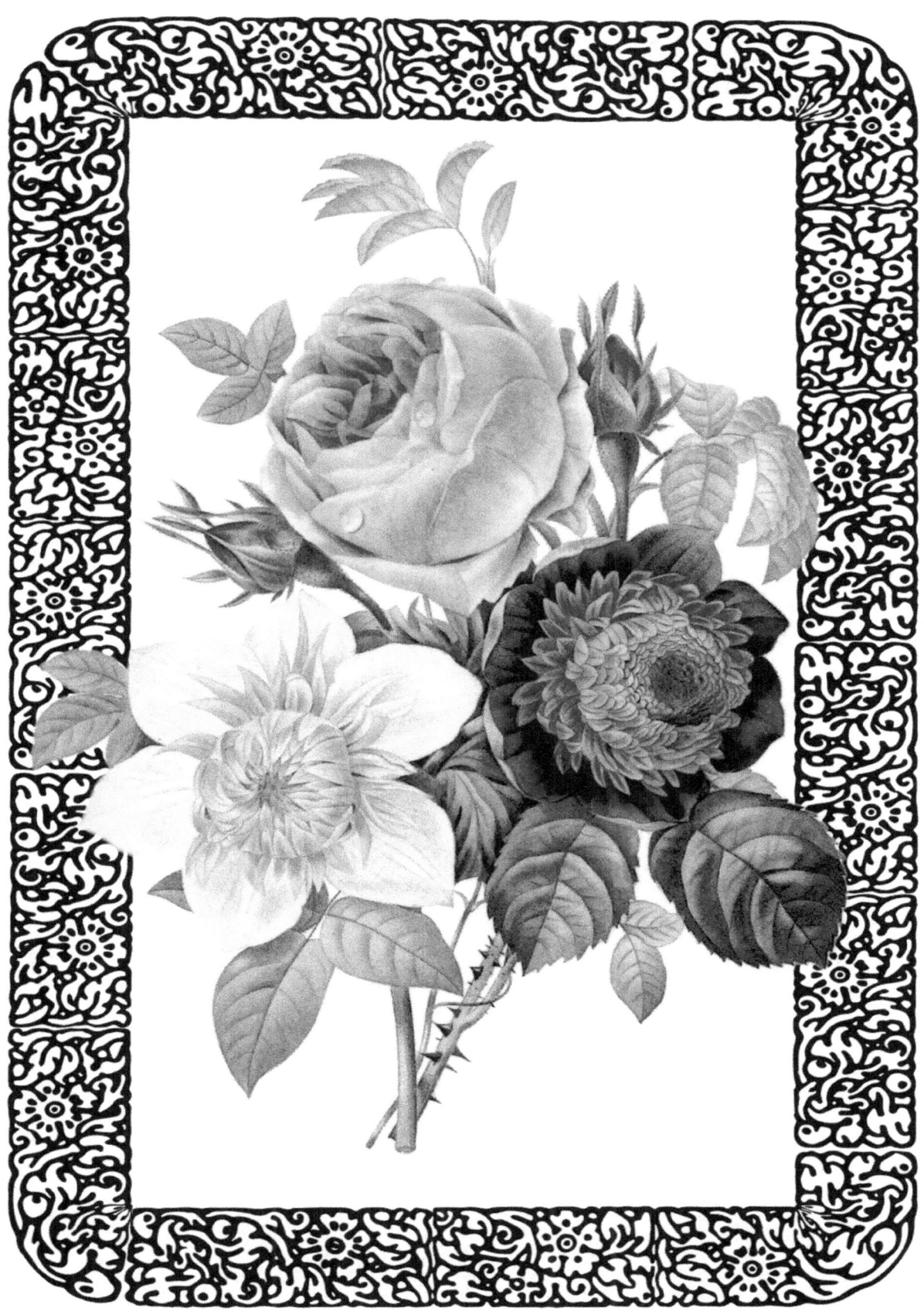